## PRESENTS

# THE DEFINITIVE GUIDE TO
# ROBLOX
## 2023

## A TOTALLY INDEPENDENT PUBLICATION

Written by Naomi Berry
Designed by Jon Dalrymple

## PBR

**A Pillar Box Red Publication**

# CONTENTS

# WELCOME MESSAGE

Welcome, Robloxians, to endless possibilities. Whether this is your first rodeo or you're a true veteran, the world of Roblox doesn't get any smaller. You could've made your account back at launch in 2006 and there's still whole unexplored Roblox realms out there that you haven't even sniffed yet.

Of course it's impossible for any guide to tell you 'how to play Roblox'; Roblox isn't that kind of game, and honestly, there isn't enough paper in the world to print out the amount of pages that would be needed for that kind of mammoth, biblical-level quest. That's kinda the magic of Roblox: there's no one way to play it. In fact, you can play it however you want - whatever you want, too. Feel like role playing as a pixie in a magical academy? Roblox's got it. Changed your mind and want to flee a mutant murderous banana? Well (weirdly enough), Roblox's still got you covered. Even if you just want to pretend to work a shift at a pizzeria, you can in Roblox.

So what's this guide for then? It's here to help you make your way around the wonderful world of Roblox. It's a vast and a little bit intimidating expanse that stretches beyond clicking that 'Launch' button, and while you might know where you want to end up, it can be difficult working out how to get there, or how to even start. This guide covers all the basics to get your Roblox knowledge up to scratch, while also picking out some key games and genres to try, and even touching a little on how to make your own game, too.

It's time to grab your controller, your keyboard, your tablet... whatever platform that will be your portal of choice into the wonderful world of Roblox. Let's play!

# THE STORY SO FAR

Development on Roblox first began back in 2003 by its co-founders, David Baszucki and Erik Cassel. Three years later, the platform was unleashed onto the public on September 1st 2006. The platform featured the ability to create and play countless user-created games across a whole spectrum of genres, all using Lua coding.

The platform grew in popularity in the 2010s, expanding onto a range of devices such as iOS and Android in 2012 and 2014, respectively. In 2015, it made its debut on Xbox One, and even went VR with Oculus Rift in 2016. But while it was definitely growing, Roblox ultimately fell short in the mainstream gaming coverage to other games that were similarly seen as 'creative' titles, like Minecraft.

Roblox may have been around for over 15 years, but it wasn't really until the recent global pandemic that it really took off. With kids forced to spend more time indoors, more and more people discovered the possibilities of Roblox - allowing players to log on, socialize and essentially experience whatever they were missing out on with friends, old and new. When restrictions started lifting again, Roblox kept riding the wave of its newfound popularity, even hosting in-game events and concerts on par with gaming giant Fortnite.

So where does Roblox go from here? With more eyes than ever on a platform that provides the tools to tailor any gaming experience, surely the only way is up, outwards, and whatever other direction means 'more'.

While Roblox officially launched in 2006, it actually first popped onto the scene in its beta version DynaBlocks in 2004. It wasn't until 2005 that it was renamed to Roblox, and the following year that it went live.

# GLOSSARY

Before you dive into the wonderful world of Roblox, it definitely helps to know your ABCs from your XDs (which isn't what you think it is, trust me). It's not like you have to learn a whole second language to be able to play, but there are a few phrases and terms that are useful to know. No worries - we'll have you speaking like a Robloxian in no time.

## 1V1:
A one-on-one game between two players. This is usually used in combat games, but can be seen in other scenarios.

## ABC:
ABC doesn't have any specific meaning, but it's a term players use to communicate. For example, if a player says 'ABC for free stuff!', someone else would respond 'ABC' to show interest. It can also be used to show that you're ready for a task in roleplay, like if someone asks 'ABC for wizard lizard king (i.e. 'Who wants to play the wizard lizard king?') and you respond 'ABC' if you're down to play.

## AFK:
AFK stands for 'away from keyboard', and is used to describe inactive players.

## B):
A smiley face with sunglasses - infinitely cooler than a regular smiley face.

## BB:
Shorthand for Brick Battle, a type of game where players use a variety of weapons to face off against each other.

## BEAMED:
Roblox slang for banned.

## BLOXXED:
A term that means the same as 'KO'ed', i.e. "you just got bloxxed by Piggy."

## COMPED:
Shorthand for 'compromised', and usually used to describe hacked Roblox accounts.

## GFX:
Shorthand for 'graphics'.

## FFA:
Shorthand for 'free for all', which refers to a game or match (usually battles) without rules, or teams, i.e. every player for themselves.

## IC:
Shorthand for 'in character'.

## HR:
Shorthand for 'high rank', usually in reference to players.

## LIMITED ITEM:
An item that is available in the avatar shop in finite quantities. They start out as regular items for a set price, but when they sell out or are taken off-sale, they become Limited. These items are deemed as collectibles and viewed as pretty valuable on the trade market.

Try On    3D

ITED

6

## Miss Scarlet

By Roblox

| | |
|---|---|
| Best Price | ⬡ **51,000** |
| | See more Resellers |
| Type | Face |
| Genres | **Town and City** |
| Description | Frankly my dear, you look ready for anything. |

Buy

Try On

LIMITED U

⭐ 144K+

# LIMITEDUNIQUE (LIMITEDU):

LimitedU items are essentially the same as Limited items, but instead of waiting for them to go off-sale, they are limited from the start. Naturally, they're also viewed as valuable and are hot commodities on the trade market.

# LMAD:

'Let's make a deal'. This is often used when players want to trade items.

# LUA:

Lua is the coding language that Roblox is built with. It's a great entry-level code for beginners as it's relatively simple compared to other coding languages. You can try it out in the Roblox Studio.

# MK:

Shorthand for 'mmokay', and usually just means 'yes'.

# MR:

Shorthand for 'mid rank', usually in reference to players.

# NFT:

Shorthand for 'not for trade', used in trading games and communities.

# NGF:

Another trading shorthand, this means 'not going first'.

# Make Anything You Can Imagine

With our FREE and immersive creation engine

Start Creating

Manage my experiences

## OBBY:

Shorthand for 'obstacle course'. These aren't your regular, playground-level obstacle courses, mind you - expect the unexpected when taking these challenges on.

## OOC:

Shorthand for 'out of character'. This is used mostly to signal real communication in role playing games.

## OOG:

Shorthand for 'out of game'. It has a pretty wide range of usage, from outside of the specific game you're playing to outside of all of Roblox, i.e., reality.

## OOF:

The iconic Roblox death sound, it's often used casually in chatting to refer to a mistake or something negative, like if someone messed up or something is too hard.

## PLOX:

Robloxian for 'please'.

## PTS:

Shorthand for 'permission to speak'. You'll likely see this in the chat sections of certain game genres, like military, naval etc.

## PS:

Shorthand for 'private server'. You can use private servers to play with friends.

## R6:

The first six-jointed avatar.

## R15:

The 15-jointed avatar successor to the R6.

## RAP:

Shorthand for 'recent average price', this is used to refer to items in trading.

## ROM:

Shorthand for 'random death match', a term used largely in fighting games.

## ROBLOX STUDIO:

Different from the gaming platform, Roblox Studio allows players to use the Lua coding to create their own objects, items, and even games. Check out this guide's Roblox Studio chapter on p. 60-61.

## ROBLOXIAN:

Any player that plays Roblox is deemed a Robloxian (hey, that's you!).

## ROBUX:

Robux is the Roblox currency for making in-game purchases. It's also sometimes referred to as 'Bobux' and 'Roux', both misspellings that grew in popularity.

## RTHRO:

The most visually-advanced avatar option. Its name is a combination of 'Roblox' and 'anthropomorphic'.

## SFL:

An acronym for 'single file line', this is often used as a command for players to arrange themselves in a game.

## STS:

Another acronym for player arrangement, but this one stands for 'shoulder to shoulder'.

## TDM:

Shorthand for 'team deathmatch', a mode featured in a lot of fighting and shooting games.

## TERMED:

Shorthand for 'terminated'.

## TOP EARNING:

Refers to the games that have made the most Robux in the past week.

## TT:

While this usually means a crying face in the real world, it actually stands for 'till tomorrow' in Roblox. Players usually use this term when signing off to say goodbye to their friends.

## WIP:

Shorthand for 'work in progress'.

## XD:

Okay, turn it on its side... see it now? Kinda? It's supposed to be a laughing face.

Spotted a term in-game that you can't find here? This glossary covers the most general terms across the platform, but we get it: sometimes you've got to get a little niche. Be sure to check out the genre pages in this guide to find more genre-specific terms and acronyms.

# AVATARS

It's not just enough to decide which of the many worlds on offer in Roblox to jump into first; you've first got to decide how you want to look while doing so.

## FROM R6...

Roblox has come a long way since its debut - do you remember its very first avatar, R6? R6 was the Roblox OG, named after its six joints (hey, it was a different time back in 2006). Okay, so R6 wasn't exactly breaking any boundaries when it came to pioneering visuals, but the Catalog did allow players to customise skin tones and shirts, before eventually adding hats, pants and facial expressions into the mix.

## ...TO R15...

If R6 was named after its six joints, it's a safe bet to assume R15 was an upgrade, motion-wise at least. R15 dropped on the scene a whole decade after R6 in 2016 (just one joint away from being a really satisfying name/joint tie-in). With over twice the joints, it also came with new animations, and the ability for players to adjust its articulations with brand new body scaling tools.

## A BLAST FROM THE PAST

If you feel like going old school, you can still use the original R6 and older R15 avatars. The Roblox team has said a core tenet of their work is to keep backward compatibility, so they won't be getting vaulted any time soon.

# ...TO RTHRO!

Thankfully the Roblox team didn't wait another decade to drop an Avatar update, as 2018 brought us its current iteration: Rthro. Rthro gives players the ability to mould their avatar however they see fit, with Rthro packages and 3D clothing allowing a wider range of customisation.

You might be surprised to hear that when the Rthro first dropped, it wasn't all that popular. It could just be an appreciation of the good old classics, but despite it being the most recent and advanced model, the Rthro isn't the overwhelmingly dominant Avatar type in game - especially since a lot of older games and environments were built to support the simpler R6s and R15s. You know, it's not always easy accommodating anthropomorphic humanoids into everything.

You can customise your avatar in the Avatar Shop at the Roblox launch page. There are premium bundles and pieces that cost Robux to purchase, but more than plenty of items are free to download and use, too.

# GENRE: BUILDING

What goes with blocks like cookies go with cream? Building, of course! The building genre is as natural a fit to Roblox as any, with tons of great titles letting you build from the depths of the world's core to the top of the highest rollercoaster.

Developed by : berezaa Games
Genre : Building
Released : June 2015

## MINER'S HAVEN

One of the most popular experiences in the building genre, Miner's Haven is an assembly line-type sandbox game, where the player is challenged to create an efficient and (most importantly) profitable ore production facility.

There's no tutorial available, so it can be a little tricky to get your head around - but practice makes perfect! It also helps if you have experience with other tycoon style Roblox games, since the basic premise is pretty much the same.

## THEME PARK TYCOON 2

Developed by : Den_S
Genre : Building
Released : January 2012

If you've ever wanted to build your dream theme park, then Theme Park Tycoon 2 is the experience for you. But it's not enough just to design the flashiest sideshows and wildest roller coasters; you've also got to turn your hand to management, and make sure your park is as profitable as it is fun.

This kind of game is in no way unique to Roblox (there have been variants on the theme park simulator since the '90s), but this version is a fun and surprisingly in-depth way to take on the tycoon classic.

# SANDBOX 1

Developed by : NullSenseStudio
Genre : Building
Released : February 2011

Often imitated, never equalled - Sandbox (1) by NullSenseStudio is the OG sandbox building game, with many copies cropping up in the community over the years. This version challenges players to build whatever they want, and is the perfect arena to show off your skills and let your imagination run wild.

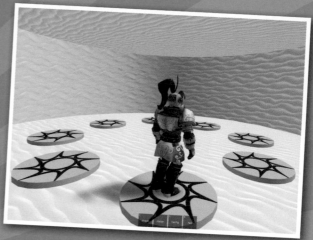

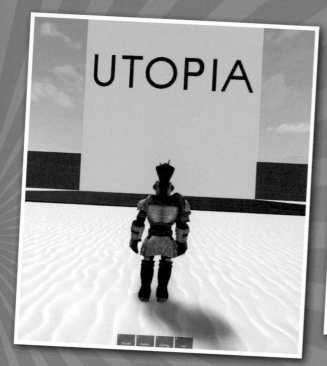

# OTHER GREAT BUILDING GAMES:

## WELCOME TO ROBLOX BUILDING

Welcome to Roblox Building
86% 148
A rewrite of "Welcome to Roblox Building", which was a sandbox buildin...

## WIZARD TYCOON 2 PLAYER

[SPELLS] Wizard Tycoon - 2 Player
87% 1.5K
NEW 2 player wizard tycoon! Work together to become the most powerful...

## AZURE MINES

Azure Mines
86% 43
You're in charge of restoring an old mining facility back to its former glory....

# GENRE: HORROR

It's no surprise that in Roblox's mammoth library of games, more than a few of them come with a good scare. It's not all sunshine and smiles over here - sometimes it's time for a good jump, scare and scream, and these horror games are some of the best the platform has to offer.

## PIGGY

Developed by : MiniToon
Genre : Horror
Released : January 2020

Piggy [BREAKOUT CHAPTER]
Do you have what it takes to escape Piggy and uncover the mysteries...

Piggy is a survival horror game where players take on the role of a police officer investigating the mysterious disappearance of George Pig. After arriving on scene, the player is suddenly knocked out cold by another pig, awakening in an unknown bedroom shortly after. From there, it's up to the player to escape before the murderous pig tracks them down and finishes the job.

This is one of Roblox's flagship horror games, filled with modes, maps, books, chapters and different endings for players to discover. It won Game of the Year in the 8th Bloxy Awards, and was the fastest Roblox experience to reach 1 billion visits just 83 days after its creation.

Murder Mystery 2
Can you solve the Mystery and survive each round? INNOCENTS...

Developed by : Nikilis
Genre : Horror
Released : January 2014

## MURDER MYSTERY 2

This experience puts the player in one of three roles: sheriff, innocent and murderer. Players are randomly assigned a role for each game, and must work together to identify the murderer... or, if they're the murderer, work alone to finish everyone off before they work out who you are...

# INSANE ELEVATOR

**Developed by :** Digital Destruction
**Genre :** Horror
**Released :** October 2019

Insane Elevator technically classifies itself as an 'All Genres' game, but it's pretty clear the overarching goal is to make you jump and its cast features some of the most iconic scary movie characters, so... horror it is.

Players have to get into an elevator for the chance to win different rewards, but there's a survival element in there, because you're likely to be joined by the likes of Pennywise the Clown, Sired Head, and other killers who'd quite like to stop you from gaining those prizes, to put it lightly. How many floors will you survive?

# OTHER GREAT HORROR GAMES:

## NANNY

Nanny [HORROR]
78%  1.7K
Hello! Welcome to Nanny. Avoid Nanny and find the exit to survive!

## STOP IT, SLENDER!

Stop it, Slender!
90%  106
While avoiding Slenderman and his elusive proxies, citizens must find all 8...

## ZOMBIE ATTACK

Zombie Attack
93%  3.3K
Welcome to Zombie Attack! Team up with your friends as you earn new...

## SURVIVE THE KILLER

Survive the Killer!
By Slyce Entertainment

Favorite  Follow  577K+  64K+

17

# ROLLERCOASTER ROYALE

Theme park tycoons are always a top pick in the building genre.
Can you find these theme park words in the wordsearch below?

| S | U | A | R | M | E | D | R | H | B | S | R | R | A |
| U | K | P | L | C | A | N | D | Y | F | L | O | S | S |
| A | N | C | A | R | O | U | S | E | L | E | F | E | R |
| A | P | U | E | F | N | S | P | T | P | E | E | T | L |
| P | A | R | A | D | E | D | L | M | D | L | T | W | F |
| B | A | L | L | O | O | N | S | O | A | T | E | K | A |
| N | U | O | O | R | T | F | U | N | H | O | U | S | E |
| R | S | R | F | E | R | R | I | S | W | H | E | E | L |
| R | B | U | A | O | P | D | U | N | K | T | A | N | K |
| O | O | I | D | B | U | M | P | E | R | C | A | T | S |
| H | A | U | N | T | E | D | H | O | U | S | E | E | T |
| E | D | C | D | R | O | P | T | O | W | E | R | O | E |
| R | R | O | L | L | E | R | C | O | A | S | T | E | R |
| U | D | P | R | A | D | E | W | A | L | T | Z | E | R |

**CANDY FLOSS**
**FUN HOUSE**
**BALLOONS**
**CAROUSEL**
**FERRIS WHEEL**
**ROLLERCOASTER**

**BUMPER CATS**
**DUNK TANK**
**PARADE**
**WALTZER**
**HAUNTED HOUSE**
**DROP TOWER**

18

Puzzle solutions on pages 62-63

# YOUR WORST NIGHTMARE!

A murderous pig, a bloodthirsty banana, a haunting ventriloquist...
Roblox has some of the most memorable and menacing horror
characters, with some of the most unique appearances. What kind
of creature would you have lurching into the Insane Elevator?

We've created one here for you to colour in!

# GENRE: TOWN AND CITY

Town and City games are pretty easy to identify because the gameplay centers around the setting of a town or city. The actual gameplay itself can vary quite a lot, but if the setting features that cityscaple skyline, it fits in here.

Town and City is definitely one of the most popular genres on Roblox, with some of the platform's most recognisable titles falling under this category. Whether it's going on a metropolis-destroying rampage or just understanding the importance of teamwork when it comes to making pizza, Town and City's got it all.

## MEEPCITY

Developed by : Alex Newtron
Genre : Town and City
Released : February 2016

MeepCity is a social hangout that's not entirely dissimilar to old school online classics like Club Penguin and Toontown Online. Players can spawn in, hangout and chat with friends and customize their homes. There's also a ton of minigames available, such as MeepCity Racing (a Mario Kart-kinda experience) and an obstacle course called MeepCity: Star Ball.

The game was the first on the Roblox platform to surpass 1 billion visits, and once held the title of most visited game of all time, before Adopt Me (see p. 44) swept in and took first place.

(see p. 44)

Developed by : Dued1
Genre : Town and City
Released : March 2008

## WORK AT A PIZZA PLACE

Work at a Pizza Place (often abbreviated to just WaaPP) is one of the platform's most iconic games. Why? It's difficult to say - it doesn't offer some of the flashier, more fantastical gameplay or concepts you can find in other experiences. But something about the simple and wholesome vibe of working together to fulfill pizza orders has kept players coming back since March 2008 - just under 4 billion times, to be exact.

Okay, so there's a little bit more to it than just making pizza. There are six positions available in the pizza parlor: Supplier, Delivery, Pizza Boxer, Cook, Cashier and Manager. The game involves role-playing elements too, with players using their work earnings from the pizza joint to upgrade and decorate their in-game home. They can also use their pizza cash to buy gear and order their character food. Oh, and if the world of the pizza making industry becomes too much, they can always bounce off to Party Island.

Sounds simple, but hey - it works. Work at a Pizza Place was the first game to reach 100 million visits on Roblox.

# BROOKHAVEN RP

Developed by : Wolfpaq
Genre : Town and City
Released : April 2020

Brookhaven RP is another Town and City experience that leans heavily on roleplay elements (what did you think the RP stands for?). This experience allows players to hangout and roleplay in Brookhaven, owning and living in amazing houses, driving the coolest cars and essentially being whoever they want to be.

It's a pretty simple game, but we've already worked out that sometimes you just can't beat a well-polished classic. It seems kids agree, as Brookhaven RP was nominated in the Favorite Video Game category at the Nickelodeon 2022 Kids' Choice Awards alongside Minecraft, Just Dance and Mario Party Superstars.

# GREENVILLE

Developed by : Greenville, Wisconsin
Genre : Town and City
Released : June 2017

Greenville is a Town and City game that offers a little more niche of a take on roleplay. This polished-looking game centers around car building, allowing players to build and customize their own ride to drive around the nearby town of Greenville.

There are a ton of different models and customization options available for players - in fact, there's more than 400 cars available to purchase, ranging from sedans and coupes to SUVs, trucks and even emergency vehicles. Players can take on jobs to earn money in order to customize their dream wheels to their heart's desire.

# DINOSAUR CITY SIMULATOR

Developed by : White Dragon Horse
Genre : All
Released : March 2021

This newer addition to the genre is technically an All Genres experience, but the gameplay is pretty city-centric. Unlike the roleplaying elements of the other games, Dinosaur City Simulator lets players explore the metropolis as a giant (or little, it's up to you), destructive dinosaur.

But it's not just about exploration - players have to take on other gigantic foes in battle, with the city being an unfortunate bystander to the fallout and destruction.

# OTHER GREAT TOWN AND CITY GAMES:

## TINY TOWN TYCOON

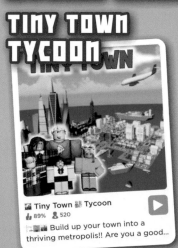

🏙️ Tiny Town 🏙️ Tycoon
👍 89%  👤 520
🏗️🏙️ Build up your town into a thriving metropolis!! Are you a good...

## ROCITIZENS

RoCitizens [Firefighter]
👍 88%  👤 1.7K
Firefighter Update + Fire station, ladder truck, and firefighter job +...

## JAILBREAK

Jailbreak [TRADING!]
👍 88%  👤 16.5K
⚠️ Thanks for your trading feedback! Expect more soon! 🔼🔼 The TRADE...

## CITY LIFE TYCOON

City Life Tycoon
By Tycoon League

# GENRE: MILITARY

Some of the most successful video games of all time are military-based, and Roblox has its own military offerings that are just as popular.

## ZEPPELIN WARS

Developed by : lolkiller101
Genre : Military
Released : May 2020

Zeppelin Wars [ALPHA 0.69G]
👍 64% 👤 311
Version: Alpha 0.69. This is still in early testing. Inspired by...

Zeppelin Wars is a newer entry in the Military genre, but has already picked up a lot of pace in the category. In this experience, players can take the battles to the skies, as they are sorted into two teams that compete on the decks of opposing zeppelins.

Choose your team

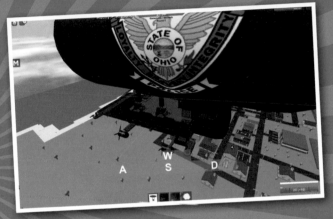

There are four modes to choose from: Classic, Raid, Skirmish and Dreadnought. This iteration of the game is heavily inspired by a 2008 experience called 'Zeppelin Battle' by myrkwarrior.

# OTHER GREAT MILITARY GAMES:

## MILITARY TYCOON

[SEA UPDATE!] Military Tycoon
👍 93% 👤 8.8K
Leave a like 👍 and favorite ⭐ for more Military Tycoon updates!...

## ARMORED PATROL 2

Armored Patrol v9.5
👍 82% 👤 174
UPDATE 4/13 - Prototype visual effects from AP2, internal framewor...

## BEDWARS

BedWars ➕ [SEASON 5!]
👍 83% 👤 69.7K
🔥🔥 Updates every Friday at 3:00pm PST, 6:00pm EST 🔥🔥 Controls:...

## BRITISH MILITARY ACADEMY

[🔥SEBEE🔥] British Military Academy
By [BA] British Army

AIR CORPS PILOT   MILITARY POLICE   DRILL INSTRUCTOR

Favorite  Follow  229K+  50K+

## BATTLESHIP BATTLE

Battleship Battle ⚓
By Scheinwerfer Studios

Favorite  Follow  97K+  15K+

# PIZZA PERFECT

Want to Work at a Pizza Place? Let's see if you've got what it takes to rise to the top and become a pizza pro.
Can you find the slices missing from a customer's order?

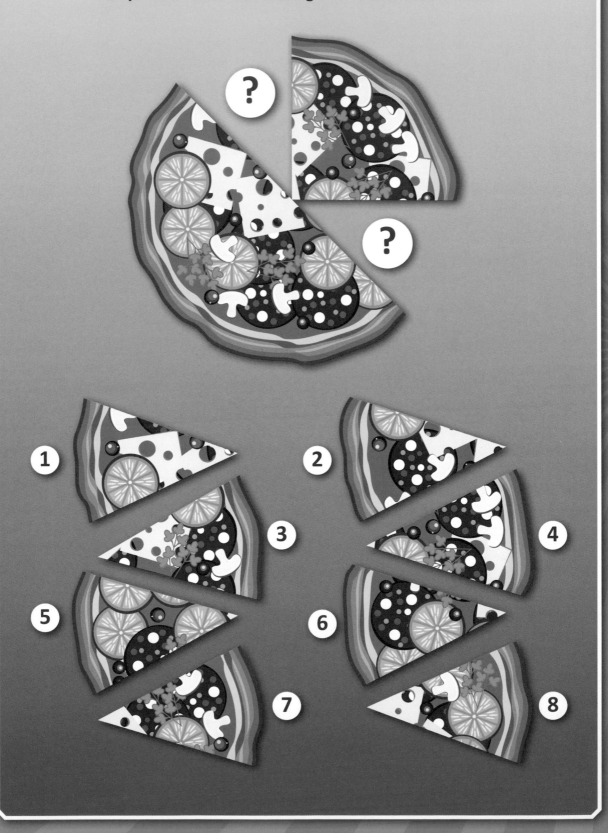

Puzzle solutions on pages 62-63

# MILITARY MIX-UP

Attention! Can you unscramble the names of these popular military games? Here's a hint - the first letter of each word is correct!

## Blcawkhka Ruesec Moissin 5
B

## Wra Siumoralt
W

## Sadnstuhr Miiatryl Amcadey
S

## Crainmil vs. Staw
C

## Pinros Ryeola
P

## Dy-ad
D

## Utin 1689
U

## Teh Cnorseqoru
T

## Aodrerm Ptluaor
A

## Nobo Aymr Toynoc
N

Puzzle solutions on pages 62-63

# GENRE: COMEDY

Comedy is quite a niche genre of gameplay, and difficult to really nail down in definition. In terms of Roblox, it generally involves things that are weird (well, weirder than the usual Roblox fare), but it also has some offerings that will genuinely work a chuckle out of you. If it's been memed, you best believe there's probably an experience of it available on Roblox.

## DEVIOUS LICK SIMULATOR

Developed by : lick.io
Genre : All
Released : September 2021

Remember that 2021 TikTok trend that had students stealing things from school - anything from pencil sharpeners to soap dispensers and stop signs? You know, that period where no school bathroom was safe. Yeah, it was definitely one of the year's darkest (and stupidest) trends, but Roblox has managed to provide a much better way to participate. Even if the trend has fallen out of favour, it's still a pretty ripe source for gameplay.

This experience prompts players to steal items and sell them for coins, advancing through floors and wreaking havoc in high school. And hey, this version of the meme doesn't involve any actual real-world vandalizing, stealing, damage or consequences, so that's always a plus.

## THE PRESENTATION EXPERIENCE

Developed by : Minimal Games
Genre : Comedy
Released : October 2021

The Presentation Experience is pretty much a 'what it says on the tin' game: players roleplay in school as students making a presentation, and others disrupt as often as they can by coughing, dancing the macarena and farting, to name but a few rambunctious methods.

You can earn points for disruption by successfully presenting, so it's a pretty simple gameplay loop set-up that can provide a few easy laughs if you feel like unplugging and playing something that doesn't require a whole lot of brainpower.

# MEGA NOOB SIMULATOR

Developed by : thunder1222
Genre : Comedy
Released : December 2019

If there's one word to describe Mega Noob Simulator, it's 'silly'. The aim is to become the biggest noob by smashing bacon hairs to grow into a literally bigger noob. Taking on Boss Bacon, a Clownfish army and other noobs in a PVP arena is the gameplay. It's just silly. But don't get us wrong - sometimes silly is just what the doctor ordered.

# OTHER GREAT COMEDY GAMES:

## STRONGMAN SIMULATOR

## WACKY WIZARDS

## ESCAPE MCDONALDS OBBY

27

# GENRE: MEDIEVAL

Medieval games throw the player way back to the usually unspecifically-dated past to get up to a bunch of historical hijinks. Whether it's wielding a sword to joust a fellow knight or to tear down a mythical beast, medieval games bring the fun with an extra side of history (accuracy not always included).

## KINGDOM LIFE II

Developed by : DevBuckette
Genre : Medieval
Released : July 2012

Kingdom Life™ II
(UNDERWORLD UPDATE)
Welcome to Kingdom Life II, where you can be virtually anything and...

Kingdom Life II is a medieval-fantasy roleplay game that allows players to create their own character to write history with. In terms of storyline, this experience is pretty open, and encourages players to test the limits of their imagination within this vast, medieval world of wizards, fairies, elves, dragons... and the odd human, too.

## MEDIEVAL WARFARE

Medieval Warfare
Four kingdoms and an outpost, an endless battle between sworn...

Developed by : Schematics
Genre : Fighting
Released : March 2013

Medieval Warfare may be technically classified as a Fighting game but come on - the name alone makes it pretty clear that it deserves a spot on this list.

This battle sim is set in a warring medieval world, with four kingdoms and an outpost in endless battle. Players can roleplay as something time-period appropriate (from a King all the way down - literally - to a miner), explore their kingdom, scour the lands for materials to craft new weapons and of course, engage in some good old medieval battle.

BATTLE

USE AN ENDLESS VARIETY OF WEAPONS TO FIGHT WITH OR AGAINST YOUR FRIENDS!

**Medieval Warfare**
By @Schematics

Unable to verify that you have access to this experience. Please try again later.

Favorite    Follow    130K+    28K+

ROLEPLAY

BE A KING, MINER, LUMBERJACK OR ONE OF THE MANY OTHER ROLES AVAILABLE TO YOU!

**Medieval Warfare**
By @Schematics

Unable to verify that you have access to this experience. Please try again later.

Favorite    Follow    130K+    28K+

# SORCERER'S AWAKENING

Developed by : FarmerJaller
Genre : Medieval
Released : May 2010

Ever wondered what Star Wars would be like if it was set in the Medieval era? Well wonder no more: Sorcerer's Awakening is the answer. This medieval fantasy roleplay game takes inspiration from the iconic Star Wars IP. It may no longer be receiving any updates, but it's still a fun experience to take on as it stands.

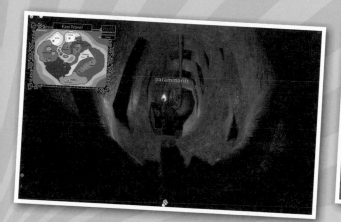

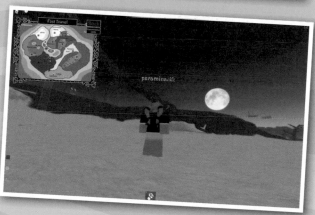

# OTHER GREAT MEDIEVAL GAMES:

## ROBBERIES! EMPIRE ROLEPLAY

[ROBBERIES!]
Empire Roleplay
By Holy Roman Empire

## BALLISTA

Ballista
[ALPHA]
By Ballista

## LIONHEARTS: CRUSADE

[DUNGEONS!]
Lionhearts:
Crusade
By Lionhearts: Crusade

# FINISH THE JOKE!

Ready to play some comedy games on Roblox? You better have your set prepared first! See if you can match the set-up with the punchline. We've given you a head start!

**1** — What do you call a nose with no person?

**2** — Why didn't the skeleton cross the road?

**3** — Why was the broom late for school?

**4** — What's the smartest dinosaur?

**5** — What does a cloud wear under its raincoat?

**6** — What did the sink say to the toilet?

**7** — What do you call a dog magician?

**A** — He overswept.

**B** — Thunderwear.

**C** — A labracadabrador.

**D** — He had no guts.

**E** — The thesaurus.

**F** — Nobody nose.

**G** — You look a bit flushed.

Puzzle solutions on pages 62-63

# MEDIEVAL MAZE

Can you avoid the dangerous dragons and warlocks to find your way out of this medieval maze?

## START HERE

## FINISH HERE

# GENRE: ADVENTURE

One of the biggest and most popular game genres on the platform is Adventure. It's probably because like a few of the other bigger categories, 'adventure' kinda covers quite a few bases, and can be an umbrella term over a lot of gameplay mechanics. You'll find titles here that overlap a little into other genres (especially RPGs), but what do they all have in common? A sense of adventure...

## ROYALE HIGH

Developed by : callmehbob
Genre : Adventure
Released : April 2017

Royale High somehow achieves the impossible: it makes you actively want to hang out at school. Okay, so it's not just any school - it does help when the school in question is an enchanted academy filled with magical creatures, and they give out diamonds for attendance.

This school-themed roleplay game started its life as a Winx Club fan roleplay (originally titled Fairies and Mermaids Winx High School), but was reworked just a few months after its debut to widen its scope to all things magical. From there, it's just gotten bigger and bigger, with nearly 7 billion visits to date.

Players can zip around campus and magical realms with their teleportation staff, earning Diamonds to use to customise their magical avatar with a ton of community-created content. The game also has a ton of great in-game events held for holidays, so be sure to check out the new activities and limited-time items around the holidays.

Developed by : HenryDev
Genre : Adventure
Released : January 2018

## TREASURE HUNT SIMULATOR

Treasure Hunt Simulator is the perfect game for anyone who's dreamed of sailing the seas in search of loot. Players can pirate to their heart's content: digging out blocks Minecraft-style, discovering buried treasure and using your found coins to upgrade your toolkit and pet companions.

It's a simple enough concept, but the game has consistent updates and new content, and has been a regular feature in the Popular section of the games page. Hey, with over 550 million visits and over 3 million favourites, it must be doing something right in its simplicity.

# LITTLE WORLD

Developed by : Counter Impact
Genre : Adventure
Released : August 2020

Little World may be one of the newer games in this list, but it certainly made a splash in the Adventure genre. This unique roleplay experience has players begin their journey as a cute little ladybug, exploring and eventually evolving their way up the food chain to become the apex predator.

There's an element of survival in there too to keep things interesting, with evil ants and bosses (including Godzilla, because... why not?) to navigate. But if survival isn't your jam, there's also mini-games, flags to capture and pets to own, too.

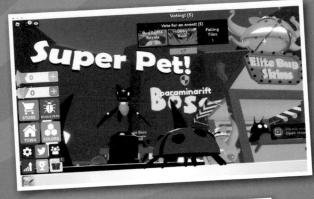

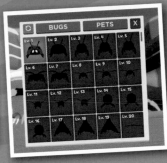

Developed by : Bloxtun
Genre : Adventure
Released : July 2009

# MEGA FUN OBBY

Mega Fun Obby is an OG - a long standing classic among the Adventure genre, for sure. If you're into platforming and parkour, then Mega Fun Obby's got you covered; this obstacle course has almost 2700 stages (and counting, the developers regularly update

this experience) for you to take on. And if you somehow manage to run your way through all they have to offer (go touch some grass, but good for you), this game has infinite replay potential, with speedrunners constantly trying to one-up each other's best course runs.

Developed by : zKevin
Genre : Adventure
Released : October 2017

# ROBOT 64

Robot 64 takes cues from classic 3D platforming titles, its biggest inspiration being Nintendo's iconic Super Mario 64 (hence the name).

Players play as the robot Beebo, exploring the world of Papatopia to collect ice cream to shoot at the sun in hopes of destroying it. You know, a very normal, logical task to do. Gameplay features the classic catalogue of platforming motions (running and jumping), as well as cracking out more modern mechanics like jetpacks to take on boss fights.

Dr. Smar
Your name is Beebo. Hear that? B-e-e-b-o. Me Smar, you Beebo.

# OTHER GREAT ADVENTURE GAMES:

## BUILD A BOAT FOR TREASURE

**Build A Boat For Treasure**
👍 93%  👤 16.2K
Build your ship and set sail for your adventure! Liked the game? Don't...

## DRIVING EMPIRE

**[25+ NEW CARS!] Driving Empire**
👍 89%  👤 7.6K
🚗"Empire Games" Group members earn 15% cash more while driving! 🚗 ...

## SCUBA DIVING AT QUILL LAKE

**Scuba Diving at Quill Lake** 🤿
👍 92%  👤 241
🤿New update! -Improved swimming controls -New water VFX -Bug fixes ...

## HIDE AND SEEK EXTREME

**Hide and Seek Extreme**
By @Tim7775

## TOWER OF HELL

**Tower of Hell**
By YXCeptional Studios

# GENRE: SCI-FI

The realm of science-fiction is as broad as it is infinite. From the cold, steel lights of a laboratory discovering new energy resources, to the bright, blinking bulbs of neon cyberpunk and the sparkling stars of space exploration - sci-fi covers a lot of bases, and the Roblox genre does too.

## NEON DISTRICT

Developed by : InfiniteEffect
Genre : Sci-Fi
Released : October 2011

Neon District (Character Codes!)
👍 91%  👤 60
Updates: 📋 Use Character Codes to customize yourself fast! ⛽ Fresh Cu...

Neon District is any sci-fi explorer's dream. Players are transported into the future, 2047, dropped on the streets of a neon-lit, cyberpunk city called Neon District.

The whole city is prime to explore, with shops open for business, restaurants ready to cook up food and even more to discover in the winding streets, both up in the towering buildings and down below in the underground waterways and sewers.

This game started out as a mere showcase build, but development has evolved this game into a full roleplay experience, with puzzling and lore hidden throughout for the player to solve and uncover.

## OTHER GREAT SCI-FI GAMES:

### INNOVATION INC. SPACESHIP

Innovation Inc. Spaceship
👍 90%  👤 118
Further than any man or machine has ever been, flies the Innovation Inc...

### SPACE SAILORS

SPACE ◆ SAILORS

SPACE SAILORS (Spaceflight & Skydiving Sim)
👍 89%  👤 271
Welcome to SPACE SAILORS! ⚡ 🏆 2021 Bloxy Nominee, an achievement to...

### PINEWOOD COMPUTER CORE

PINEWOOD COMPUTER CORE

Pinewood Computer Core
👍 84%  👤 63
Explore a secret underground facility that's about to explode! Your mission ...

# SPOT THE DIFFERENCE

Can you spy the eight differences between these two screenshots from Royale High?

Puzzle solutions on pages 62-63

# LAB TESTS

The lab is a popular backdrop in sci-fi games, so maybe you can help out with a few experiments. Can you work out which beaker will fill up with chemicals first?

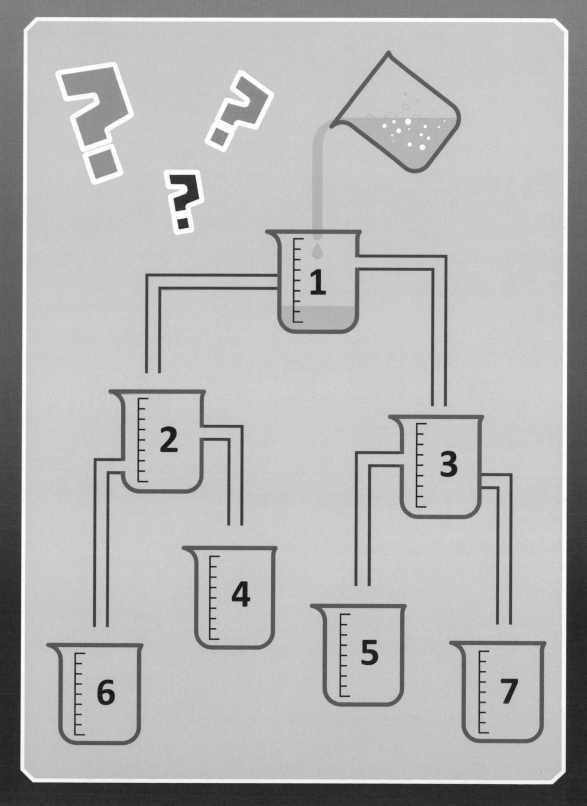

# GENRE: NAVAL

It's time to take it to the seas! Whether your vessel is a battleship, the Flying Dutchman or even a submarine, there's plenty of picks in the naval genre for you to get your feet metaphorically wet.

## PIRATE WARS

Developed by : Pudinzo
Genre : Naval
Released : August 2010

Pirate Wars!
Welcome to Pirate Wars! Pirate Wars 2 is in development, it will be released here...

A trip on a pirate ship is the quintessential Roblox naval experience, and Pirate Wars is one of the best ways to do so. It's been around for over a decade and it's still going strong - that's how you know it's a good 'un.

This game pits players in two teams of pirates against each other, all in the name of treasure (of course). Pick the right side of swashbucklers and fight for your island's glory in an epic battle of the seas, cannonballs at the ready!

## OTHER GREAT NAVAL GAMES:

### TRADELANDS

**Tradelands**
👍 83%  👤 74
Become a wealthy merchant or the world's most fearsome pirate: the choic...

### BATTLESHIP BATTLE!

**Battleship Battle** ⚓
👍 86%  👤 125
Dive into the midst of destruction on the high seas! Experience the brutal...

### PILFERING PIRATES

**Pilfering Pirates**
By @Pseudosuper

⭐ Favorite    📶 Follow    👍 135K+    👎 25K

# GENRE: FPS

First Person Shooters (FPS for short) have always dominated the video game market with an iron fist. Some of the biggest games of all time are from this genre, or at least borrow key gameplay mechanics or elements from it. Roblox FPS offerings are no different, with some of the platform's most popular and well-critiqued games being FPS experiences.

## PHANTOM FORCES

**Developed by : StyLiS Studios**
**Genre : FPS**
**Released : August 2015**

Phantom Forces [May Update]
Thank you for supporting us for over five years to help reach 1B+ visits! [Update...

When it comes to FPS, Phantom Forces is about as classic as you can get (the fact that it's inspired by genre heavyweights like Battlefield 4 should clue you in). Gameplay centers around two main factions: the Phantoms and the Ghosts. There are six game modes for players to try out: Team Deathmatch, Flare Domination, King of the Hill, Capture the Flag, Kill Confirmed and Hard Point. Other modes can also make an appearance (either on a VIP server or for a seasonal event), so there's plenty of classic FPS action to unpack for genre newbies and vets alike. It's clear that Phantom Forces is doing FPS right, as evidenced by its impressive like-to-dislike ratio, over 1.2 billion visits and long-standing spot on the Roblox front page.

**Developed by : ROLVe Community**
**Genre : FPS**
**Released : August 2015**

## ARSENAL

Arsenal
Race to the top through a massive Arsenal of weapons! Conquer the day i...

This is another experience that takes some inspiration from a Triple A shooter (this time being Valve's Counter-Strike: Global Offensive). Arsenal is an FPS with a hint of pandemonium: every time a player gets a kill (or even an assist), their weapon gets swapped out for something else. And when the weapon arsenal ranges from pistols and SMGs to bananas and Christmas baubles, there's definitely potential for things to get a little chaotic.

With three Bloxy awards under its belt (including the coveted top prize, Game of the Year), this is definitely one of Roblox's best FPS offerings and worth checking out, if only to work out how to weaponise the pocket potassium.

FPS isn't the only abbreviation used in this genre. Here are some genre-specific shorthands that you may come across in-game:

CTF - Capture the Flag    FFA - Free for All
KC - Kill Confirmed    KotH - King of the Hill
TDM - Team Deathmatch

# BIG PAINTBALL

Developed by : BIG Games
Genre : FPS
Released : July 2019

Not all takes on the FPS genre take themselves super seriously. If you want to try an entry that's a little more colourful, then Big Paintball is definitely the FPS for you. Play as a team across a variety of maps for 15 minute matches to tag your opponents.

It's a simple concept but there are a ton of different paint-wielding weapons to collect and battle abilities to unlock (via tag streaks), like radar, sentries and even drones. There are different game modes on offer too, so the replay factor is pretty high with this colourful experience.

Developed by : Metaverse Team
Genre : FPS
Released : January 2021

# NERF STRIKE

The name should give away that this game's weapon of choice is the IRL classic Nerf gun, right? Players can wield the dart blaster in three different game modes: Domination, Team-Based and Free for All. In Domination, two teams fight for control of capture points. For Team-Based, it's a simple enough premise: if you get hit with a dart, you get tagged out, and a team loses when its respawn counter hits zero. For the third mode, Free for All, players rack up individual scores based on tags they score.

NERF Strike serves up all the good old summertime backyard/street fun, but without having to worry about the weather playing nice.

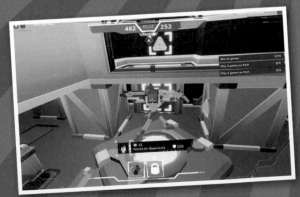

**Developed by : Bad Business**
**Genre : FPS**
**Released : May 2019**

# BAD BUSINESS

Bad Business is essentially Roblox's answer to FPS titan Call of Duty: Modern Warfare; it's a classic FPS through and through. The experience is known for its glossy cosmetics, in-depth progression system and wide array of weaponry available to wield. Fans of Bad Business should be sure to keep an eye out online - this experience has a lot of codes published to enhance gameplay.

# OTHER GREAT FPS GAMES:

## COUNTER BLOX

## SHOOT OUT

**Counter Blox**
82% · 3.5K
Take part in a 5v5 team based fire fi... across a variety of maps spanning...

**Energy Assault**
84% · 1.2K
30/05/2022 - All owned skins shown in customise - Bushes can no longer be...

[HEROES & VILLAINS] SHOOT OUT!
80% · 309
NEW SEASON: HEROES & VILLAINS
PLEASE FAVORITE US ☆ 700...

OLDSCHOOL! Island Royale!
82% · 80
UPDATE TIME! OLD RECOIL HAS RETURNED! OLD CAMERA...

## ENERGY ASSAULT

## ISLAND ROYALE

# TREASURE MAP DISASTER

Sailing the seven seas is a popular way to get through the Naval genre, but you can't do it without a map! Can you work out which pieces go where to repair the treasure map?

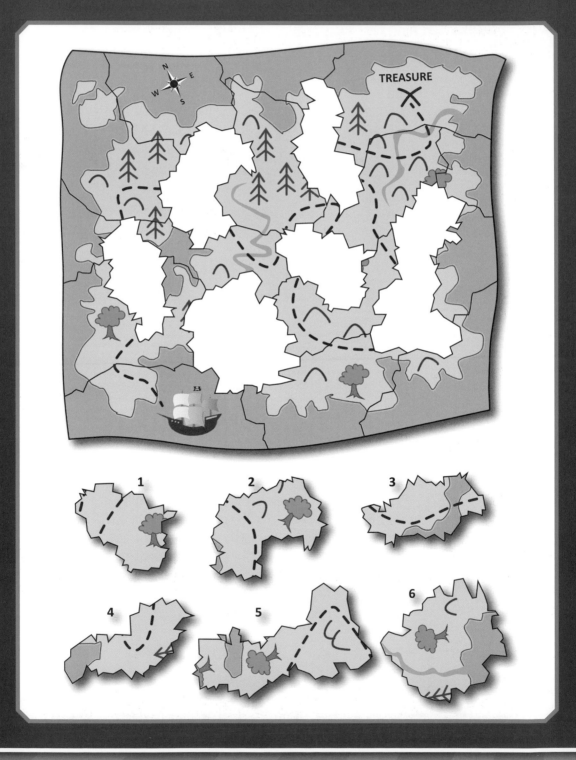

Puzzle solutions on pages 62-63

# CROSSHAIR MATCH-UP

It's time to set your aim - can you find out which target each crosshair is ready to find?

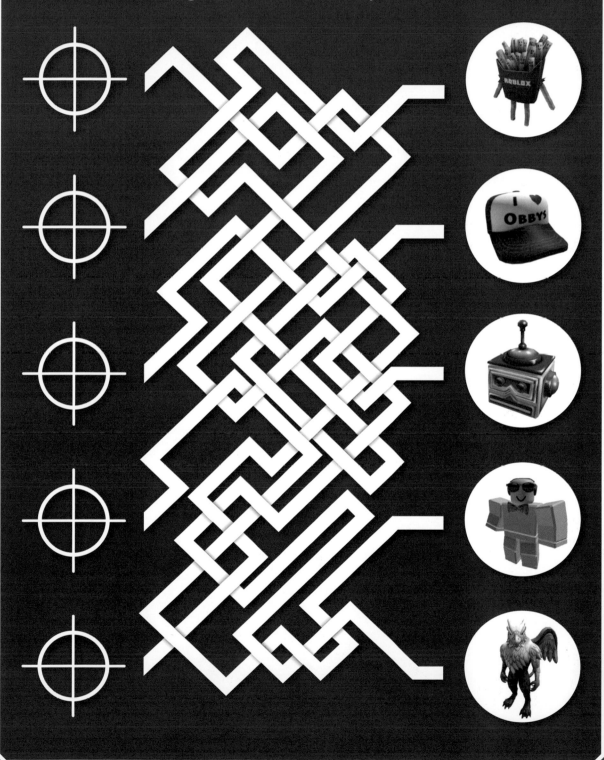

# GENRE: RPG

While most games have the player take on the part of a character, a Roleplay Game (RPG) differs in that the roleplay is the central focus over any other game mechanic. RPGs allow the player to take a walk (or Naruto run) in the life of someone completely different or even unwaveringly similar to themselves. That's the whole experience.

Some of the most popular Roblox games are classed as RPGs, and range from the arguably mundane of pretending you own a pet, to becoming a tycoon in some of your favorite Disney universes and full on open world fantasy. Here are some of the platform standouts.

Developed by : Uplift Games
Genre : RPG
Released : July 2017

# ADOPT ME!

Adopt Me! is one of the biggest games on the Roblox platform. This MMO boasts some seriously impressive numbers, like being played nearly 30 billion times by January 2022.

So what's the game all about? Adopt Me! is an adoption sim, where the player can adopt and care for a variety of different pets. These pets range in rarity (common, uncommon, rare, ultra-rare and legendary) - we're talking anywhere from a common pup to the legendary diamond dragon.

Once a pet hatches from its egg, it passes through six growth stages:

Newborn → Junior → Pre-teen → Teen → Post-teen → Full-grown

Four fully grown pets of the same type can be combined into a Neon pet, and then four fully grown Neon pets can be combined into the ultimate Mega-Neon pet. Players can also earn in-game cash for each pet they raise, which can then go back into purchasing new pets, spoiling the ones you already have, or decking out your home.

# WORLD // ZERO

Developed by : RedManta Studios
Genre : RPG
Released : August 2019

World // Zero
94% 4.6K
TOWER 4 - The next tower is now available in WORLD 8! - NEW TOWER...

If you're into Japanese RPGs and classic MMOs, then World // Zero is the Roblox RPG for you. Not only does the art style take obvious notes from anime, the gameplay does too: players can pick a starter class (something that determines a character's skill set) and battle their way through quests, dungeons and bosses throughout seven different worlds, developing their character's battle prowess and rare loot collection along the way.

[UPDATE] Shindo Life
93% 27.4K
Welcome to Shindo Life. Explore vast worlds, play many game modes...

Developed by : RELL World
Genre : All
Released : January 2020

# SHINDO LIFE

Okay, so it's not officially Naruto for legal reasons, but if it looks like Naruto, vibes like Naruto, and runs like Naruto...

To be clear, Shindo Life is technically classed as an 'All' genre title, but it has a super popular RPG Mode that allows players to take on the role of a Naruto-esque lead, complete quests, level up and explore vast worlds inspired by the iconic anime series. It even has time-based item spawns like a classic MMO.

# OTHER GREAT RPG GAMES:

## VESTERIA

Vesteria
91% 1.1K
A casual fantasy MMORPG with man open worlds to explore. Fight enemi

## WORLD OF MAGIC

World of Magic
World of Magic
92% 130
This game is currently being completely remade into Arcane Odyssey, and won'...

Heroes Online
94% 130
Welcome to Heroes Online, a game inspired by the hit series My Hero...

## HEROES ONLINE

UPDATE! Dungeon Quest! UPDATE!

UPDATE! Dungeon Quest!
91% 3.5K
Bonus Boss at the end of Northern Lands on Nightmare Difficulty. This bos...

## DUNGEON QUEST

# GENRE: SPORTS

Sports games on Roblox largely fall into the obby category, but there's more than a few good shakes at the more traditional sports, too.

Developed by : AUDIO80
Genre : Sports
Released : February 2019

# WIPEOUT OBBY

It's no surprise that Wipeout Obby is the most played in the Sports genre - this game gives players the chance to fulfill the ultimate dream: try out the infamous Wipeout course. And it's even better because you don't have to put your actual, real body through the likely trauma.

This obby has all the iconic obstacles from the TV show: the swings, the sweeper, and of course, the big balls. Players can try their best to maneuver their avatar through the course to win a bunch of prizes. Oh, and if you run it a few times and think you're pretty decent, why not have a go at beating some of the official speedrun entries? Current world records are set at around two minutes and 40 seconds.

# KICK OFF

Developed by : CM Games
Genre : Sports
Released : November 2015

On a platform with bloodthirsty bananas and gravity-defying obbys, Kick Off keeps it clean, summed up quite succinctly by its description: "A soccer game simplistic so everyone can enjoy." And trust us - they're not exaggerating here. You can shoot, slide tackle ancd sprint.  Hey, sometimes you just want to play it clean and classic, and that's what Kick Off is here to provide.

# DODGEBALL!

Developed by : Alex Newtron
Genre : Sports
Released : February 2015

**DODGEBALL**

DODGEBALL!
👍 K15 👤 11
Your friends PWN you in Dodgeball!
PWN them in ROBLOX Dodgeball! Figh...

Waiting for 2 or more players

CHOOSE YOUR CHARACTER

ALEXNEWTRON PRESENTS

Loading Assets

It's time to crank out the five D's of dodgeball: dodge, duck, dip, dive and dodge - it's time for dodgeball. Players can fight in teams (the classic red v. blue) for basic victories, but also earn cool skill achievements like ricochet KOs, game winning MVP, perfect aim and a Godlike, no-hit run.

# OTHER GREAT SPORTS GAMES:

## SUPER STRIKER LEAGUE

### PHENOM

PHENOM

**Phenom**
👍 77% 👤 287

Click the Question Mark in game to learn the controls needed to play! Recent...

**Super Striker League**
👍 75% 👤 2.4K

This is soccer / football... but amped up to the extreme! ⚽ 👟 Take the field and...

### NIKELAND

NIKELAND
2x XP

By Nike

UNLEASH SPORTS SUPERPOWERS.
WHERE SPORT HAS NO RULES

Favorite   Follow   35K+   7,288

47

# GOTTA ADOPT 'EM ALL

RPG Adopt Me! is one of the biggest games on Roblox, but it looks like the amount of pets on offer might have gotten a little out of hand... Can you count how many different pets there are?

Puzzle solutions on pages 62-63

# SPORTS SPORTS SPORTS

Roblox's sports genre is as varied as the real thing. Can you solve the clues and fill out this sports themed crossword?

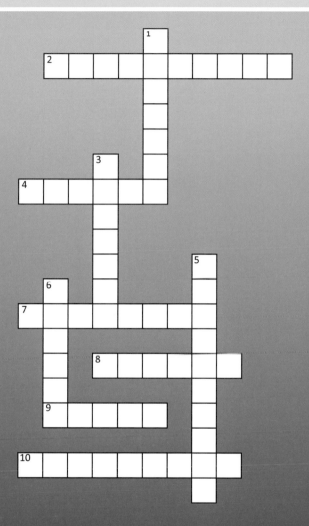

## Across

**2.** Luckily you don't have to be 6 foot tall to excel in this sport on Roblox. (10)

**4.** The genre is full of games requiring four wheels. (6)

**7.** This sport is one of the most popular types featured in the genre. (8)

**8.** This sport is featured in top sports titles like HHCL Lobby. (6)

**9.** There are a ton of American Football games on Roblox, but over in the UK, we call it something else. (5)

**10.** Dodge, duck, dip, dive and dodge.(9)

## Down

**1.** En garde! (7)

**3.** So it's not technically a sport in the real world, but it certainly is in Roblox! It does have really big, red, bouncy balls, after all. (7)

**5.** Thanks to Roblox, we can hit the beach and play this whatever the weather. (10)

**6.** According to our American friends, this is the real name of the beautiful game. (6)

Puzzle solutions on pages 62-63

# GENRE: FIGHTING

Fighting has long been one of the most popular genres of video games, from the early days of Virtua Fighter to more recent numbered entries in long-living series like Tekken and Mortal Kombat. So it's no surprise that Roblox has its own offering of fighting games, too. While they may not be as sophisticated as some of the big blockbuster triple A games, they can be just as entertaining.

## ANIME FIGHTERS SIMULATOR

Developed by : Sulley
Genre : Adventure
Released : January 2021

This experience may be classed as an Adventure game, there's no doubt that Anime Fighters Simulator is a fighting game at heart. Just look at the name: it's not called Anime Adventurers Simulator, is it?

But hey, its adventuring elements are what make Anime Fighters Simulator a really unique fighting game experience. Sure, players can unlock new fighters with a variety of rarities and train them to fight against others in anime battles, but it's not as simple as just doing some arcade battles or buying some DLC to access them. Players have to explore different anime-inspired worlds based on titles like Dragonball Z and Naruto in order to find new fighters and build their dream roster.

## OTHER GREAT FIGHTING GAMES:

### CRIMINALITY

[LAST SLAYERS] Criminality
75%  1.3K
V1.4.3 - Current update is experimental for the weekend...

### MUSCLE LEGENDS

Muscle Legends
86%  7.6K
Unleash your strength and become the strongest ROBLOXian of all time...

[UPDATE] Super Power Fighting Simulator
92%  1.6K
...in your body, fists, mind and ...d in this ultimate training game...

### SUPER POWER FIGHTING SIMULATOR

Iron Man Simulator 2 [BETA]
94%  918
The sequel to Iron Man Simulator by ...rphos! Controls: Q = Call suit E =...

### IRON MAN SIMULATOR 2

# GENRE: WESTERN

Yeehaw! It's time to take a trip to the wild, wild west in the world of Roblox. It may not be the biggest category on the platform, but there's definitely some stellar representatives of the genre in there. Saddle up!

Developed by : Starboard Studios
Genre : All
Released : September 2018

## THE WILD WEST

Does it get any more western than The Wild West? This action-packed experience throws players back to the golden days of the American Frontier. There are two paths to walk (or ride, I suppose): live by the law by hunting down bounties or living peacefully in the town, or wreaking havoc as an outlaw and robbing banks, stealing loot, and even terrorizing innocent civilians.

It's a wild world, so keep an eye out whichever path you choose - and not just for other players, there are bears out there too!

## OTHER GREAT WESTERN GAMES:

### WESTBOUND

Westbound
👍 86%  👤 2.8K
☀ Spring Update: -UI has also been upgraded and a tutorial has been adde...

### 2 PLAYER HEIST TYCOON

Two Player Heist Tycoon
👍 79%  👤 0
NEW: Added new map, new gear and a bounty system! Note: I've reverted to t...

### HORSE VALLEY LEGACY

Horse Valley
Legacy
By @SirMing

⭐ Favorite   📶 Follow   👍 82K+   👎 20K+

# GENRE: ALL

When the only limitation in Roblox is your own imagination, of course not all games will fit neatly into specific categories. Lots of games span a bunch of different gameplay styles, combining both similar and disparate genres together to create one-of-a-kind experiences that are truly unique to Roblox. Some games aren't meant to be categorized, and here are some of the highlights.

# NATURAL DISASTER SURVIVAL

Developed by : StickmasterLuke
Genre : All
Released : March 2008

Natural Disaster Survival
90% 11.6K
Quickly, run around in circles! Your life depends on it!

This round-based game forces players to use the most natural of human instincts: survival. When a round begins, players are given around 30 seconds to prepare for one of 12 possible natural disasters: flash floods, tornados, thunderstorms, fires, meteor showers, tsunamis, blizzards, sandstorms, acid rain, earthquakes, deadly viruses and volcanic eruptions.

There are 21 possible maps, which vary from beachsides and ranches to raceways and rocket launch sites, to name a few. While you may know your map, you won't know what the incoming disaster will be until it hits. There are general clues you can spy when preparing, like the colour of cloud linings or the sound of wind. General tip? Don't automatically go for the highest ground - if it's a fire, tornado or earthquake, you'll be out pretty quickly.

[Update 3.5 🏴‍☠️] King Legacy
91% 22.8K
Join Dis for more code Level Cap: 3400
There are 36 Physical Fruits In-Game -...

Developed by : Venture Lagoons
Genre : All
Released : December 2019

# KING LEGACY

King Legacy is an anime-based experience based on the iconic manga series, One Piece. In fact, the game was originally called King Piece, but had to change for copyright reasons.

Still, name or no name, the popularity of One Piece certainly carried over, as King Legacy is one of the platform's most popping experiences. Players can sail the open seas as a marine or pirate, gaining rank and power, and gathering different types of devil fruits to eat in order to gain special abilities.

# PET SIMULATOR

Developed by : BIG Games
Genre : All
Released : January 2021

Also known as PSX, this game is essentially Roblox's answer to Pokémon, but crossed with a pet sim. Players can collect coins, buy eggs and hatch them to get a whole range of pets - from cute and cuddly to... uh, alien parasites. As the player progresses, new worlds and biomes are unlocked to explore.

If you want to play this game, be sure to check online for codes! The developers, BIG Games, often post new codes that can provide a whole bunch of bonuses, like boosting the number of eggs you can hatch, getting free diamonds, and even making the rarer and more elusive pets easier to track down.

# OTHER GREAT ALL GENRE GAMES:

## ALL STAR TOWER DEFENSE

## TOWER DEFENSE SIMULATOR

[2x XP] All Star Tower Defense
92% 20.5K
Use your units to fend off waves of enemies. Each Unit has Unique Co...

UPDATE 26

[UPD] Clicker Simulator!
95% 23.6K
NEW CODE AT 525K LIKES! LIKE THE GAME (Use last code unlock...

Tower Defense Simulator
94% 13.8K
In this world, no one can survive alone. Team up with friends to fend off...

LIMITED!
Mega Mansion Tycoon [2 NEW CARS!]

Mega Mansion Tycoon [2 NEW CARS!]
93% 22.4K
NEW UPDATE!! Food and dishes ...ns 2 NEW cars LIMITED...

## CLICKER SIMULATOR

## MEGA MANSION TYCOON

# ROBLOX X REAL WORLD

With the massive boom in attention that came to Roblox over the last few years, it was no surprise that real world industries started looking to the platform to collaborate. It makes sense that as a platform that caters to everyone, Roblox's roster of collaborators is... pretty varied, to say the least. What did Hello Kitty, the Grammys, McLaren F1, Gucci and Chipotle have in common before 2020? Nada. Zilch. Realms apart. But after 2020? Well...

## THE ROBLOX GRAND STAGE

2020 was a big year for Roblox in a lot of ways, but one of its biggest mainstream coverage events was when rapper Lil Nas X held the platform's first virtual concert. This wasn't the first time a game had held a concert (after all, Fortnite had been boasting similar events), but it was the first time a major music artist went outside the ubiquitous battle royale. Lil Nas X debuted his Christmas song Holiday to an audience of around 33 million over four shows.

The Lil Nas X Concert Experience was just the beginning. The next year, American band Twenty One Pilots took to the Roblox stage. The duo promoted their album Scaled and Icy in one of the biggest events for Roblox in 2021. The five song concert drew in attendees from over 160 countries, and allowed the audience to dictate the setlist by voting on the next song. Since then, Roblox has hosted Concert Experiences with Tai Verdes and 24kGoldn.

But Roblox doesn't stop at concerts. They've got a whole spectrum of live music events covered where artists can debut new music to Robloxian fans while they chill and hang with their friends. In 2021, Roblox hosted the Zara Larsson Dance Party, a virtual concert event to celebrate the deluxe version of the singer's Poster Girl album. The Swedish popstar left her mark on the game as a purchasable bundle in the Avatar Shop, along with other avatar merch and emotes inspired by her music.

Roblox then followed up with a new feature called Listening Parties. The first act to test it out was pop singer Poppy with her LP Flux. She was then followed by global DJ David Guetta popping into the metaverse for a slick DJ set in 2022, American boyband Why Don't We, and Italian hip hop singer Achille Lauro, to name but a few.

Roblox has even become a platform for big music events like awards shows. Awards shows were out there gasping their last collective breath, relying on dwindling TV ratings like it's still the 90s. This is the 21st century, and Roblox could provide a modern solution for a modern problem. Shows like the BRIT Awards, the Logitech Song Breaker Awards and even the Grammys made their debut on Roblox in 2022, bringing an industry's traditional celebrations to a brand new audience.

**Couldn't make it live? Don't worry - all of the Roblox concert experiences are available to watch back on the official Roblox YouTube channel.**

# ROBLOX GOES FASHION

Roblox collaborated with one of the world's leading fashion houses, bringing the Gucci Garden exhibit to the virtual world. While the exhibition toured the real world, Roblox players were able to experience the house's 100th year anniversary celebration via a virtual Gucci Garden space for two weeks in May 2021. Players took on the appearance of a neutral mannequin as they became immersed with the elements of the Archetypes exhibition. The Garden also hosted a store with exclusive limited-edition avatar items up for grabs.

But it's not just the high fashion houses that are testing out the metaverse. Nike made their debut in the world of Roblox via NIKELAND, an experience where sport has no rules. The game invites players to create the future of sports, in a land inspired by the brand's real life headquarters. Games like tag, the floor is lava and dodgeball all feature unique accelerometers, encouraging players to use real life movement to enhance their in-game results. NIKELAND also features a digital showroom to kit out your avatar in a special collection of Nike shoes, clothes and accessories.

The fashion world returned to Roblox with Ralph Lauren: the Winter Escape, Vans World, and even hosted the Fashion Awards 2021 with the British Fashion Council. The fashion industry seems pretty committed to increasing accessibility and making new advancements in the metaverse, so who knows which big names will pop up on the platform next?

# ROBLOX AND THE SILVER SCREEN

The television and film industry has long been a fan of Roblox, but the last few years really saw some of its heaviest hitters taking advantage of Roblox's surge in popularity.

Since 2020, Roblox has collaborated with movies such as DC's Wonder Woman 1984 and Lin Manuel Miranda's blockbuster musical In the Heights. The smaller screen also made its appearance on the platform, perhaps best showcased in the appearance of Netflix's smash hit series Stranger Things. Fans of the nostalgic cult classic can log in to Roblox and hang out at the iconic Starcourt Mall, and even try their hand at escaping Hawkins Lab.

A lot of these special collaborations were limited time events, but a few are still available to explore. While some of their special items and features were time-locked, you can still play a lot of the experiences. Check out My Hello Kitty Cafe and Stranger Things: Starcourt Mall.

This is your Hello KittyCafe Truck! Let's start with the basics and learn how to

## MASCOT MADNESS

You know your platform has made it when Her Royal Highness, eternal icon Hello Kitty graces it with her presence. After opening numerous real world locations in the United States and across Asia, Sanrio launched their very first virtual cafe game in Roblox in Spring 2022.

My Hello Kitty Cafe is a simulation RPG, allowing players to manage their own truck and pop-up cafe while recruiting some of Sanrio's most popular characters. Sanrio stated that they plan on massively expanding their metaverse presence over the next year or two, so it makes perfect sense that Roblox would be the site of their very first step.

# ROBLOX IN NUMBERS

Sure, we've heard a million times already how Roblox sky-rocketed in 2020, but do we really understand how big the platform became over the last few years? It's time to boil down some of Roblox's successes into cold, hard numbers, big enough to make you go oof.

Roblox has nearly 55 million daily active users. **55 MILLION**

**200 MILLION** And around 200 million people log in to play every month.

In fact, there's a good chance that there are about 1.5 million players live on Roblox right now, as you read this. **1.5 MILLION**

 If Roblox's 55 million daily users were a country, it'd be bigger than Canada. And more than twice as big as Australia!

The platform houses more than 40 million games. **40 MILLION**

**9.5 MILLION** And those 40 million games need developers, right? About 9.5 million of them, to be exact.

It's literally impossible for someone to play all the games available in the current catalog. Playing even just one minute of each game would take 40 million minutes in total, which is just over 76 years - and that's not including time for eating or sleeping. **40 MILLION MINUTES**

**5.7 MILLION** At its ultimate peak, Roblox boasted a huge 5.7 million concurrent users. That's not far off the entire population of Singapore.

# 1.92 MILLION

Which game holds the record for the most concurrent users? That'd be Adopt Me! with 1.92 million concurrent players in April 2021.

An average Robloxian spends about 2.6 hours per day on the platform.

# 2.6 HOURS

**25%**

**72%**

**3%**

When it comes to splitting between devices, there's a clear winner. About 72% of Roblox usage is done via mobile, with 25% done via desktop and only 3% via game console.

In fact, Roblox is so popular on mobile that it has a total of almost 500 million downloads on mobile alone.

# 500 MILLION

# 830,824 TIMES

And that 3% on consoles is still impressive! Roblox was downloaded 830,824 times in just its first month on Xbox One.

The first Roblox Concert Experience with Lil Nas X was watched 33 million times over four shows in only one weekend.

# 33 MILLION

# 26 MILLION

The annual Bloxy Awards are also huge draws, with the 2021 ceremony drawing in over 26 million visits in total.

# $100,000 (USD)

And it's all for a good cause: in 2020, the Bloxy Awards raised $100,000 (USD) for charity.

# ROBLOX STUDIO

So you've played your way through the 100 or so games that we've recommended, as well as others you found along the way. Now what? Well, what about turning your hand to creating your own game?

Don't have any previous game development experience? No problem. Roblox Studio is a creation engine designed to help anyone - literally, anyone - start from wherever they need to, and finish with a Roblox game to call their very own.

Roblox Studio is available on both PC and Mac.

## GETTING STARTED

Launching up Roblox Studio should look something like the image below. From here, you can choose from a bunch of premade templates to use as the basis of your game - including village and Capture the Flag, to name a few. If this is your first dip in Roblox Studio, we recommend trying out the Obby template to get your bearings; it's a classic game type with a pretty basic form that's perfect to sharpen your developing tools. Oh, and they're pretty widely played too, which always helps

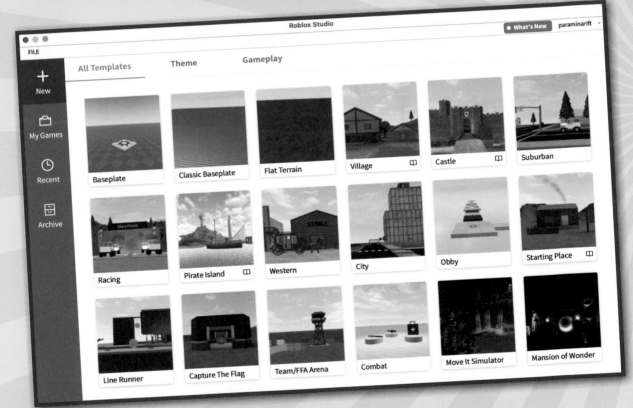

## CREATING AND EDITING

Developers recommend a two-button mouse with a scroll wheel for the easiest experience using Roblox Studio.

Okay, so let's say we went with the Obby template. From here, you'll find yourself in a much more intimidating looking window, full of options and drop-down menus. Don't panic! It's actually pretty easy to understand the more you look at it. The most important thing is the window in the middle - you can use this interface to edit the game's environment. Plain speak? This is what the game's going to actually look like. From here, you can click, drag and edit components to your heart's content.

With the template, key game mechanics like start and end points are already in place, with a bunch of pre-generated obstacles. You can make whatever adjustments you want, like playing with the lighting (which includes changing with the skybox).

It may seem like an overwhelming process just now, but it's definitely something you'll get used to the more you play around in it. Take some time to explore the different menus and see what each slider does - the more you discover and learn, the more you can apply to your own build.

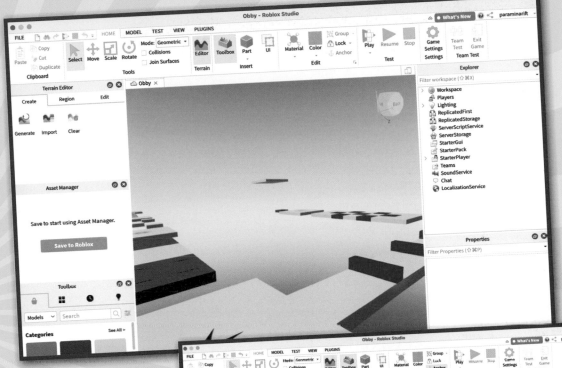

If you want to get a bit more ambitious and start something from scratch, it's always a good idea to check out more in-depth information on the official Roblox Studio guide at https://developer. roblox.com/en-us/ onboarding.
This comprehensive guide has everything you'll need, it even takes you through basic and intermediate coding and modeling to bring your creation to life.

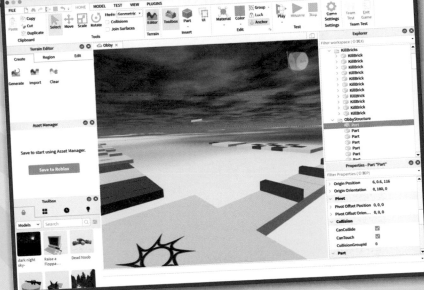

## PUBLISHING TO ROBLOX

If you're done tinkering, it's time to go live! Simply hit File > Publish to Roblox. There's a few little admin things to add in, like a name, description, icon, genre etc. Once that's done, you're all set to play your own creation - and even have others have a go, too!

# ANSWERS

## P.18: ROLLERCOASTER ROYALE

| S | U | A | R | M | E | D | R | H | B | S | R | R | A |
|---|---|---|---|---|---|---|---|---|---|---|---|---|---|
| U | K | P | L | C | A | N | D | Y | F | L | O | S | S |
| A | N | C | A | R | O | U | S | E | L | E | F | E | R |
| A | P | U | E | F | N | S | P | T | P | E | E | T | L |
| P | A | R | A | D | E | D | L | M | D | L | T | W | F |
| B | A | L | L | O | O | N | S | O | A | T | E | K | A |
| N | U | O | O | R | T | F | U | N | H | O | U | S | E |
| R | S | R | F | E | R | R | I | S | W | H | E | E | L |
| R | B | U | A | O | P | D | U | N | K | T | A | N | K |
| O | O | I | D | B | U | M | P | E | R | C | A | T | S |
| H | A | U | N | T | E | D | H | O | U | S | E | E | T |
| E | D | C | D | R | O | P | T | O | W | E | R | O | E |
| R | R | O | L | L | E | R | C | O | A | S | T | E | R |
| U | D | P | R | A | D | E | W | A | L | T | Z | E | R |

CANDY FLOSS
FUN HOUSE
BALLOONS
CAROUSEL
FERRIS WHEEL
ROLLERCOASTER
BUMPER CATS
DUNK TANK
PARADE
WALTZER
HAUNTED HOUSE
DROP TOWER

## P.24: PIZZA PERFECT

## P.25: MILITARY MIX UP

1. Blackhawk Rescue Mission 5
2. War Simulator
3. Sandhurst Military Academy
4. Criminal vs. Swat
5. Prison Royale
6. D-Day
7. Unit 1968
8. The Conquerors
9. Armoured Patrol
10. Noob Army Tycoon

## P.30: FINISH THE JOKE

1. F
2. D
3. A
4. E
5. B
6. G
7. C

## P.31: MEDIEVAL MAZE

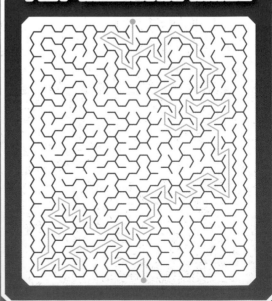